NO BAKE

COOKIES, BARS & PIES

120 Fast, Easy & Delicious Recipes

Printed in the United States of America
by G&R Publishing Co.

Distributed By:

507 Industrial Street
Waverly, IA 50677

ISBN-13: 978-1-56383-219-2
ISBN-10: 1-56383-219-4
Item #7011

TABLE OF CONTENTS

NO BAKE COOKIES

Chow Mein Clusters

Makes 2 dozen

2 C. butterscotch
  chips
2 C. chow mein
  noodles

1 C. salted peanuts

In a double boiler over simmering water, melt the butterscotch chips, stirring frequently until smooth. Remove from heat and stir in chow mein noodles and peanuts. Drop by teaspoonfuls onto waxed paper. Refrigerate until firm.

Honey Nutters

Makes 4 dozen

16 graham crackers
1 C. crunchy peanut butter
⅔ C. honey

½ C. powdered milk
1 C. shredded coconut

Crush the graham crackers in a food processor or between 2 pieces of wax paper using a rolling pin. In a large mixing bowl, combine peanut butter, honey and powdered milk. Mix well. Stir in crushed graham crackers. Make small balls with dough and place on waxed paper. Roll balls in shredded coconut.

Peanut Butter Dreams

Makes 4 to 5 dozen

½ C. butter, softened
4 C. powdered sugar
2 C. creamy peanut butter

3 C. crispy rice cereal
2 C. chocolate chips
4 T. shortening

In a large mixing bowl, combine butter, powdered sugar, peanut butter and crispy rice cereal. Mix well. Roll mixture into small balls and set aside. In a small saucepan over low heat, melt chocolate chips and shortening. Remove from heat. Coat the balls in the chocolate mixture. Refrigerate for several hours before serving.

The Original

Makes 4 dozen

2 C. sugar
3 T. cocoa powder
½ C. margarine
½ C. milk
Pinch of salt

3 C. old-fashioned
  rolled oats
½ C. peanut butter
1 tsp. vanilla

   In a large saucepan, bring sugar, cocoa powder, margarine, milk and salt to a rapid boil for 1 minute. Add oats, peanut butter and vanilla. Mix well and remove from heat. Working quickly, drop by teaspoonfuls onto waxed paper and let cool.

Mountain Cookies

Makes 2 dozen

2 C. sugar
½ C. milk
¼ C. butter
3 T. cocoa powder

3 C. old-fashioned
  rolled oats
½ C. shredded coconut
½ C. peanut butter
1 T. vanilla

   In a large saucepan over medium high heat, combine sugar, milk, butter and cocoa powder. Bring mixture to a boil, stirring frequently, until sugar is completely dissolved. Mix in oats, shredded coconut, peanut butter and vanilla. Stir until well combined and drop dough by tablespoonfuls onto waxed paper and let cool.

Peanut Butter Chews

Makes 3 dozen

1 C. corn syrup
1 C. sugar
1 C. creamy peanut
   butter
4½ C. corn flakes
   cereal

1 C. chocolate chips,
   optional
1 C. butterscotch
   chips, optional

In a large saucepan over medium heat, combine corn syrup and sugar. Bring to a boil for 1 minute and remove from heat. Stir in peanut butter until well blended. Mix in corn flakes cereal until evenly coated. Drop by spoonfuls onto waxed paper. In a microwave-safe bowl or double boiler, melt chocolate chips and butterscotch chips, stirring often until smooth. Drizzle melted chocolate over cookies.

Fruit & Nut Cereal Clusters

Makes 2 dozen

1 (12 oz.) pkg. white
baking chips
1 C. dried fruit, such
as cranberries,
raisins, diced
apricots

2 C. rice and corn
cereal squares
¼ C. peanuts

In a large microwave-safe bowl, heat white chocolate chips in microwave, stopping to stir every 30 seconds, until completely melted. Gently stir in fruit, cereal squares and peanuts. Mix until well coated. Drop by tablespoonfuls onto waxed paper. Refrigerate for 1 hour. Cover and store in refrigerator.

Eskimo Snowballs

Makes 2 dozen

1 C. margarine or
  butter, softened
1 tsp. vanilla
6 T. cocoa powder
1½ C. sugar

4 C. quick oats
Powdered sugar
Shredded coconut
Chopped nuts

In a medium bowl, cream softened butter, 4 tablespoons water and vanilla. Add cocoa powder, sugar and oatmeal and mix well. Roll mixture into 1″ balls. If necessary, add more water to make dough stick together. Roll half of the balls in powdered sugar and coconut and the other half in chopped nuts.

Almond Cookies

Makes 4 dozen

24 oz. almond bark
2 C. Honey Nut
  Cheerios cereal

2 C. crispy rice cereal
2 C. peanuts

In a microwave-safe bowl, melt almond bark on high, about 2 to 3 minutes, until soft and creamy. Add Cheerios, crispy rice cereal and peanuts. Stir until completely mixed. Drop by teaspoonfuls onto waxed paper. Cookies will firm as they cool.

Java Bites

Makes 3 dozen

2 C. finely crushed
   sugar cookies
1 C. finely chopped
   hazelnuts, toasted*
1⅓ C. powdered
   sugar, sifted,
   divided

¼ C. light corn syrup
2 T. coffee flavored
   liqueur
2 T. butter, melted

In a medium bowl, combine crushed cookies, toasted hazelnuts, 1 cup powdered sugar, corn syrup, coffee flavored liqueur and melted butter. Stir until well mixed. Shape mixture into 1″ balls. In a shallow bowl, place remaining ⅓ cup powdered sugar. Roll balls in powdered sugar until completely coated and let stand for 2 hours. If desired, roll balls again in powdered sugar right before serving. Chill in refrigerator for 2 days or freeze up to 3 months.

To toast, place chopped hazelnuts in a single layer on a baking sheet. Bake at 350° for approximately 10 minutes or until hazelnuts are golden brown.

Orange Fingers

Makes 4½ dozen

3½ C. crushed vanilla
  wafer cookies
2¾ C. powdered
  sugar, sifted
1½ C. chopped
  pecans

1 (6 oz.) can frozen
  orange juice
  concentrate,
  thawed
½ C. butter, melted
1 (7 oz.) pkg.
  shredded coconut

In a large bowl, combine crushed vanilla wafer cookies, sifted powdered sugar and chopped pecans. Mix well. Stir in orange juice concentrate and melted butter. Shape dough into 2″ fingers. Roll in shredded coconut and refrigerate.

Wonderful White Chocolate Cookies

Makes 2 dozen

2 C. white baking chips

½ C. chunky peanut butter

1½ C. miniature marshmallows

1 C. unsalted peanuts

1 C. Cheerios cereal

Melt white baking chips in microwave or a double boiler. Remove from heat and stir in peanut butter. Stir in marshmallows, peanuts and cereal. Drop by teaspoonfuls onto waxed paper. Let cool, cover and store in refrigerator.

Chocolate Whiskey Truffles

Makes 2 dozen

8 oz. chocolate chips
½ C. butter
⅔ C. finely crushed gingersnap cookies

3 T. whiskey
½ C. cocoa powder
½ C. powdered sugar

In a medium saucepan over low heat, melt chocolate chips and butter, stirring until smooth. Mix in crushed gingersnap cookies and whiskey. Pour mixture into a large bowl. Cover and chill until firm, about 45 minutes. Line baking sheets with foil. Drop truffle mixture by tablespoonful onto the foil. Freeze for 15 minutes. Remove from freezer and roll each truffle into smooth rounds. Into a shallow bowl, sift cocoa powder and powdered sugar. Roll each truffle in the cocoa mixture. Cover and refrigerate in an air-tight container. Let stand for 15 minutes at room temperature before serving.

Holiday Wreaths

Makes 10 to 12 wreaths

46 large
marshmallows

½ C. butter

1½ tsp. green food
coloring

3½ C. corn flakes
cereal

Red cinnamon
candies

In a large saucepan over low heat, melt marshmallows and butter. Add food coloring and mix until dark green. Gently fold in corn flakes. Drop by teaspoonfuls onto waxed paper. If desired, arrange cookies into wreath shapes. Place cinnamon candies on wreaths and chill in refrigerator.

Jimmy Carter Cookies

Makes 2 dozen

⅔ C. sugar
⅔ C. light corn syrup
1 tsp. vanilla

1¼ C. chunky peanut butter
3 C. corn flakes cereal

In a large saucepan over medium heat, combine sugar and corn syrup. Bring to a boil and add vanilla and peanut butter. Stir until well mixed. Gently mix in corn flakes. Drop by tablespoonfuls onto waxed paper. Cookies will harden as they cool.

Oatmeal Cocoa Macaroons

Makes 2 dozen

¾ C. butter
½ C. milk
2 C. sugar
½ C. shredded
  coconut

3 C. old-fashioned
  rolled oats
½ C. cocoa powder

In a saucepan over medium heat, combine butter, milk and sugar. Stirring constantly, bring mixture to a boil. Continue to boil and stir for 2 minutes. Remove from heat and add coconut, oats and cocoa powder. Stir until well mixed. Drop by teaspoonfuls onto waxed paper. Chill macaroons in refrigerator.

Caramel Nut Clusters

Makes 2 dozen

¼ C. butter or margarine

½ lb. (approximately 28) caramels, wrappers removed

2 T. milk

3½ C. corn flakes cereal

½ C. chopped peanuts

½ C. shredded coconut

In a large saucepan over low heat, combine butter, caramels and milk. Stir until melted and smooth. Remove from heat and add corn flakes, chopped peanuts and coconut. Mix well. Drop by tablespoonfuls onto waxed paper. Cookies will harden as they cool.

Rum Balls

Makes 4 dozen

1 (11 oz.) pkg.
  chocolate wafer
  cookies, finely
  crushed
1½ C. finely chopped
  pecans

½ C. light corn syrup
¼ C. light or dark
  rum
½ C. powdered sugar

In a large bowl, combine crushed chocolate wafer cookies and chopped pecans. Mix well, and stir in corn syrup and rum. Mix until well combined. Place powdered sugar in a shallow dish. Roll cookie mixture into 1″ balls and roll balls in powdered sugar. Be sure to generously coat balls in powdered sugar as they tend to absorb a lot.

Chocolate Peanut Butter Balls

Makes 4½ dozen

1 C. crunchy peanut
  butter
¼ C. margarine,
  softened
1 C. powdered sugar

2 C. crispy rice cereal
54 miniature muffin
  paper cups
1½ C. chocolate chips
2 T. shortening

In a large mixing bowl, beat peanut butter, softened margarine and powdered sugar at medium speed. Add crispy rice cereal and mix until thoroughly combined. Roll mixture into 1″ balls. Place one ball in each paper cup. Refrigerate. In a small saucepan over low heat, melt chocolate chips and shortening, stirring constantly. Spoon 1 teaspoon melted chocolate into each paper cup. Refrigerate until firm. Cover and store in refrigerator.

Crunchy Chocolate-Butterscotch Drops

Makes 2 dozen

½ C. chocolate chips
1 C. butterscotch
chips

1 C. dry roasted
peanuts
2 C. Crispix cereal

In a large heavy saucepan, melt chocolate chips and butterscotch chips over low heat, stirring constantly. Remove from heat and stir in peanuts and Crispix cereal. Drop by tablespoonfuls onto waxed paper. Cover and store in refrigerator.

Nut & Fruit Chocolate Drops

Makes 3 dozen

1 (12 oz.) pkg. chocolate chips
¾ C. coarsely chopped cashews, almonds or macadamia nuts

¾ C. raisins
½ C. dried cranberries or chopped dried apricots

In a double boiler over simmering water, melt chocolate chips, stirring until smooth. Remove from heat. Stir in nuts, raisins and cranberries. Drop chocolate mixture by teaspoonfuls onto waxed paper. Let cool until firm, about 2 hours.

Pecan Cookie Turtles

Makes 2½ dozen

30 miniature
  chocolate chip
  cookies or
  other miniature
  cookies

1 (9 oz.) pkg.
  caramels, wrappers
  removed

2 C. pecan halves

1 C. chocolate chips

¼ C. chopped pecans,
  optional

Line 2 baking sheets with waxed paper and coat with nonstick cooking spray. Arrange miniature cookies on waxed paper. In a large microwave-safe glass measuring cup, combine caramels with 4 teaspoons water. Microwave, uncovered, on high for 30 seconds. Stir and microwave for an additional 15 seconds. Top each cookie with ½ teaspoon caramel mixture. Press 4 pecan halves into caramel to resemble turtle feet. Place chocolate chips in a microwave-safe bowl or double boiler. Microwave for 1 minute or heat over stovetop, stirring often, until melted. Stir until smooth. Spoon 1 teaspoon chocolate over each cookie. If desired, sprinkle some chopped pecans over chocolate. Refrigerate at least 45 minutes before serving.

Honey Crispies

Makes 2 dozen

3 C. corn flakes cereal
1 C. powdered sugar
1 C. honey
1 C. peanut butter

1 C. raisins
1¾ to 2 C. shredded coconut

Line a baking sheet with waxed paper. In a large bowl, combine corn flakes, powdered sugar, honey, peanut butter and raisins. Mix well. Shape mixture into 1″ balls. Roll in shredded coconut. Place on prepared baking sheet and refrigerate for 1 to 2 hours, until firm.

Tumbleweeds

Makes 2 dozen

1 (12 oz.) can salted peanuts

1 (7 oz.) can potato sticks

3 C. butterscotch chips

3 T. peanut butter

In a large bowl, combine peanuts and potato sticks and set aside. In a microwave-safe bowl, combine butterscotch chips and peanut butter. Microwave for 1 to 2 minutes, stirring every 30 seconds, until melted. Pour melted mixture over peanut mixture. Stir to coat evenly. Drop by tablespoonfuls onto waxed paper. Refrigerate until set, about 15 minutes.

Bird Nests

Makes ½ dozen

3 T. butter or
   margarine
3 C. miniature
   marshmallows
4 C. chow mein
   noodles

Small jelly beans,
M&M's or other
small candies

Line a baking sheet with waxed paper. In a large saucepan, melt butter and marshmallows over medium heat, stirring until smooth. In a large bowl, combine chow mein noodles and melted marshmallow mixture. Stir until noodles are well coated. Roll mixture into 6 round balls. Place balls on prepared baking sheet. With the back of a teaspoon, press center of each ball to make an indentation. Let nests set until firm. Fill each nest with small jelly beans or other small candies like M&M's, gumdrops or chocolate covered peanuts.

Cathedral Windows

Makes 2 to 3 dozen

½ C. margarine
1 (12 oz.) bag
  chocolate chips
1 C. chopped walnuts

1 (10.5 oz.) bag
  colored miniature
  marshmallows
¾ C. shredded
  coconut

In a double boiler, melt margarine and chocolate chips over low heat, stirring occasionally, until melted and smooth. Let cool slightly. In a large bowl, combine chopped walnuts, colored marshmallows, and melted chocolate mixture. Sprinkle five 9″ sheets of waxed paper generously with shredded coconut. Divide dough into five sections and place one section on each sheet of waxed paper. Roll dough tightly into 2″ diameter logs and refrigerate overnight. Before serving, unwrap logs and cut into ½″ slices.

Crunchy Caramel Cookies

Makes 2 dozen

3 T. butter or margarine

2½ C. miniature marshmallows

2 C. pretzel sticks, coarsely broken

12 caramel candies, unwrapped

2 T. peanut butter

In a heavy saucepan over low heat, melt butter. Add marshmallows and stir until smooth. Remove from heat and mix in broken pretzel sticks until lightly coated. Drop by tablespoonfuls onto waxed paper. In a heavy saucepan over low heat, melt caramels and 1 tablespoon water, stirring frequently, until smooth. Add peanut butter and mix until well combined. Drizzle mixture over pretzel drops. Let cool until firm.

NO
BAKE
BARS

Scotcheroos

Makes 1 dozen

1 C. corn syrup
1 C. sugar
1 C. peanut butter
6 C. crispy rice cereal

1 C. chocolate chips
1 C. butterscotch chips

Grease a 9 x 13″ pan and set aside. In a large saucepan over medium heat, combine corn syrup and sugar until mixture begins to boil. Remove from heat. Stir in peanut butter and crispy rice cereal. Press mixture into greased pan. In a microwave or double boiler over simmering water, melt chocolate chips and butterscotch chips, stirring often until smooth. Spread melted chocolate over cereal mixture. Cool in refrigerator until firm, about 15 minutes. Cut into squares.

S'mores Squares

Makes 1 dozen

¾ C. light corn syrup
3 T. butter
1 tsp. vanilla
1 (11.5 oz.) pkg. milk
chocolate chips

9 C. or 1 (12 oz.) pkg.
Golden Grahams
cereal

3 C. miniature
marshmallows

Grease a 9 x 13″ pan and set aside. In a medium saucepan over medium heat, combine corn syrup, butter, vanilla and milk chocolate chips, stirring constantly, until boiling. In a large bowl, place Golden Grahams cereal. Pour chocolate mixture over Golden Grahams cereal and toss until well coated. Fold in marshmallows. Spread mixture into greased pan. Let stand for 1 hour. Cut into 2″ squares.

Salted Nut Roll Bars

Makes 1 dozen

**1 (14 oz.) can
sweetened
condensed milk
1 (10 oz.) pkg. Reese's
peanut butter chips**

**3 C. miniature
marshmallows
1 (16 oz.) jar salted
or dry roasted
peanuts, divided**

In a microwave-safe bowl, combine sweetened condensed milk, peanut butter chips and marshmallows. Microwave for about 2½ minutes, stirring often, until melted. Spread half of the peanuts into a greased 9 x 13″ pan. Spread marshmallow mixture over peanuts. Top with remaining peanuts. Refrigerate for 1 hour before cutting into bars. Store at room temperature.

Special K Bars with Chocolate Frosting

Makes 18 servings

1 C. white corn syrup
1¾ C. sugar, divided
1 C. peanut butter
6 C. Special K cereal

3 T. butter or margarine
3 T. milk
½ C. chocolate chips

In a large saucepan, combine white corn syrup and 1 cup sugar. Bring to a boil and add peanut butter. Stir in Special K cereal and transfer to a greased 11 x 14" pan. In a separate bowl, combine butter, milk and remaining ¾ cup sugar. Bring to a boil, stirring constantly, and add chocolate chips. Mix well until smooth. Pour over ingredients in pan. Let cool and cut into squares.

Twix Bars

Makes 1 dozen

1 (16 oz.) pkg. Club
  crackers
1 C. graham cracker
  crumbs
¾ C. brown sugar
½ C. sugar
⅓ C. milk
½ C. margarine
⅔ C. peanut butter
1 C. chocolate chips

Place 1 layer of Club crackers on the bottom of a greased 9 x 13″ pan. In a large saucepan over low heat, combine graham cracker crumbs, brown sugar, sugar, milk and margarine. Let boil for 5 minutes. Pour mixture over crackers in pan. Cover with another layer of Club crackers. In a microwave or double boiler, melt peanut butter and chocolate chips, stirring often until smooth. Pour melted chocolate mixture over top layer of Club crackers. Refrigerate and cut into bars.

Rocky Road

Makes 1 dozen

2 C. chocolate chips
1 C. peanut butter

4 C. miniature marshmallows

Grease a 9 x 9″ pan and set aside. In a medium saucepan over low heat, melt chocolate chips and peanut butter, stirring, until completely melted. Remove from heat and stir in marshmallows. Pour mixture into prepared pan. Let cool in refrigerator before cutting into squares.

Chocolate Puffed Wheat Squares

Makes 16 servings

8 C. puffed wheat cereal	**¼ C. brown sugar**
3 T. cocoa powder	**⅓ C. butter or margarine**
⅓ C. corn syrup	

Grease a 9 x 9″ pan and set aside. In a large bowl, place puffed wheat cereal and set aside. Grease the rim of a medium saucepan to prevent boil over. In the saucepan, combine cocoa powder, corn syrup, brown sugar and butter. Cook over medium heat, stirring often, until mixture comes to a full boil. Allow to boil for 1 minute before removing from heat. Pour chocolate mixture over puffed wheat and stir until evenly coated. Using a greased spatula, press mixture into the prepared pan. Allow to cool before cutting into squares.

Mocha Java Bars

Makes 15 servings

¾ C. butter, softened, divided

½ C. sugar

1 tsp. vanilla

1 egg

2 C. graham cracker crumbs

¾ C. shredded coconut

½ C. finely chopped walnuts

2 tsp. instant coffee granules

2 T. hot strong brewed coffee

2½ C. powdered sugar

¼ C. cocoa powder

2 T. milk

6 oz. white chocolate

In a microwave or double boiler over low heat, heat ½ cup butter, sugar, vanilla and egg, stirring often until melted, thickened and well combined. Add graham cracker crumbs, shredded coconut and chopped walnuts. Mix well and transfer mixture to a greased 9 x 13" baking dish. Spread evenly and let cool. Meanwhile, to prepare filling, in a medium bowl, dissolve instant coffee granules in strong brewed coffee. Add powdered sugar, cocoa powder, remaining ¼ cup butter and milk. Mix well and spread filling over layer in baking dish. To make topping, in a microwave or double boiler over low heat, melt white chocolate, stirring often until smooth. Spread melted white chocolate over filling layer in baking dish. Let cool in refrigerator before cutting into bars.

Crunchy Fudge Sandwiches

Makes 2 dozen

2 C. butterscotch
chips
1 C. creamy peanut
butter
8 C. crispy rice cereal

2 C. chocolate chips
4 T. butter or
margarine
1 C. powdered sugar

Grease a 9 x 13″ baking dish and set aside. In a large saucepan over medium heat, melt butterscotch chips and peanut butter, stirring frequently, until smooth. Stir in crispy rice cereal. Press half of the mixture into the bottom of prepared pan. In a double boiler, melt chocolate chips and butter, stirring occasionally. Mix in powdered sugar and 2 tablespoons water, stirring until smooth. Spread chocolate mixture evenly over cereal layer in pan. Top with remaining half of cereal mixture and press down lightly. Cover and refrigerate for about 1 hour before cutting into squares.

Yummy Chocolate Oat Bars

Makes 2 dozen

1 C. butter
½ C. brown sugar
1 tsp. vanilla

3 C. quick oats
1 C. chocolate chips
½ C. peanut butter

Grease a 9 x 9″ pan and set aside. In a large saucepan over medium heat, melt butter. Stir in brown sugar and vanilla. Mix in oats. Cook over low heat for an additional 2 to 3 minutes or until ingredients are well blended. Press half of mixture into the bottom of prepared pan. In a small saucepan over low heat, melt chocolate chips and peanut butter, stirring frequently until smooth. Pour chocolate mixture over crust in pan and spread evenly. Crumble remaining half of oat mixture over chocolate layer, pressing in gently. Cover and refrigerate 2 to 3 hours or overnight. Let sit at room temperature before cutting into small bars.

Honey Nut Cereal Bars

Makes 16 bars

½ C. sugar
½ C. honey
½ C. peanut butter

3 C. Cheerios cereal
1 C. salted peanuts, optional

Grease a 9 x 13″ pan and set aside. In a large saucepan over medium heat, stir together sugar and honey. Bring to a boil and remove from heat. Stir in peanut butter until well blended. Add cereal and peanuts and mix well. Press into prepared pan. Allow to cool and harden before cutting into bars.

*Cheerio &
M&M Bars*

Makes 1½ dozen

4 T. margarine
1 (10.5 oz.) pkg.
  miniature
  marshmallows

½ C. peanut butter
5 C. Cheerios cereal
1 C. M&M candies

Grease a 9 x 13″ baking dish and set aside. In a large microwave-safe bowl, microwave margarine for 45 seconds or until melted. Add marshmallows and stir to coat. Return to the microwave for an additional 1½ minutes, stirring after 45 seconds. Mix in peanut butter and immediately stir in Cheerios. Add M&M's and mix well. Transfer mixture to prepared pan and press down with a greased spatula until evenly spread. Allow to cool before cutting into squares.

Peanut Butter Cup Bars

Makes 4 dozen

10 graham crackers
⅔ C. butter, melted
2 C. powdered sugar

1 C. crunchy peanut butter
2 C. chocolate chips

Line the bottom of a 10 x 15″ jellyroll pan with graham crackers. In a medium bowl, cream together melted butter, powdered sugar and peanut butter until smooth. Spread mixture over graham crackers and chill until firm, about 15 minutes. In microwave or a double boiler, melt chocolate chips, stirring frequently. Spread melted chocolate over layer of chilled peanut butter mixture. Refrigerate until firm and cut into squares. Place bars between layers of waxed paper in an air-tight container in refrigerator.

Funky Frito Bars

Makes 3 dozen

1 (14.5 oz.) bag of
   corn chips, slightly
   crushed
1 C. sugar
1 C. light corn syrup
1 C. creamy peanut
   butter

11 (1.55 oz.) milk
   chocolate bars or
   1½ (11.5 oz.) pkgs.
   milk chocolate
   chips

In a greased 10 x 15″ jellyroll pan, place corn chips. In a medium saucepan over medium heat, bring sugar and corn syrup to a boil. Remove from heat and stir in peanut butter until smooth. Pour mixture over corn chips and spread evenly. Place chocolate bars in a single layer over hot mixture and let melt for a few minutes before smoothing chocolate out to form a thin layer. Let cool before breaking into pieces.

Chocolate Chip Crispies

Makes 2 dozen

1 C. corn syrup   **8 C. crispy rice cereal**
1 C. sugar   **1 C. chocolate chips**
1½ C. peanut butter

Grease a 9 x 13″ pan and set aside. In a large microwave-safe bowl, combine corn syrup, sugar and peanut butter. Microwave on high until mixture begins to boil, about 2 to 3 minutes. Remove from microwave and stir in crispy rice cereal and chocolate chips until well coated. Pour mixture into prepared pan. Press down with a greased spatula until smoothed. Let cool before cutting into squares.

Chewy Chocolate Peanut Bars

Makes 4 dozen

1 C. corn syrup
¾ C. peanut butter
1½ C. chocolate chips
1 tsp. vanilla

2½ C. quick oats
1¾ C. unsalted peanuts

In a medium saucepan over medium heat, combine corn syrup, peanut butter and chocolate chips. Bring to a boil, stirring constantly. Continue to boil for 5 minutes. Remove from heat and stir in vanilla, oats and peanuts. Turn onto a greased 10 x 15″ jellyroll pan. Let mixture slightly cool before pressing down into pan. Refrigerate overnight. Let stand for 20 minutes before cutting into squares.

Crispy Butterscotch Bars

Makes 2 dozen

3 T. butter or margarine
1 (10.5 oz.) pkg. marshmallows

3 T. instant butterscotch pudding mix
6 C. crispy rice cereal

In a large saucepan over low heat, melt butter. Add marshmallows and stir until completely melted. Remove from heat. Stir in butterscotch pudding mix. Add crispy rice cereal, stirring until completely coated. Using a greased spatula, press mixture evenly into a greased 9 x 13″ pan. Let cool before cutting into 2″ squares. Serve immediately.

Cherry Mash Bars

Makes 16 servings

2 T. butter
1 C. sugar
¼ tsp. salt
⅓ C. half n' half
1 C. miniature
  marshmallows

1 C. cherry baking
  chips
1 C. chocolate chips
½ C. peanut butter
1 C. roasted Spanish
  peanuts

Line an 8 x 8″ or 9 x 9″ square pan with waxed paper and set aside. In a medium saucepan, combine butter, sugar, salt and half n' half. Heat until boiling, stirring occasionally. Boil for 5 minutes, being sure to stir often enough to keep from scorching. Remove from heat and stir in marshmallows and cherry baking chips. Press mixture into prepared pan. In microwave or double boiler, melt chocolate chips and peanut butter, stirring frequently until smooth. Mix in roasted Spanish peanuts. Spread chocolate mixture over mixture in pan. Refrigerate 2 hours before cutting into squares.

Babe Ruth Bars

Makes 18 servings

1 C. peanut butter
1 C. white corn syrup
½ C. brown sugar
½ C. sugar

6 C. corn flakes cereal
1 C. chocolate chips
⅔ C. peanuts

In a large saucepan over medium heat, combine peanut butter, corn syrup, brown sugar and sugar. Cook, stirring occasionally, until smooth. Remove from heat and quickly mix in corn flakes, chocolate chips and peanuts until evenly coated. Press entire mixture gently into a greased 9 x 13″ baking dish. Allow to cool completely before cutting into bars.

Butterfinger Bars

Makes 2 dozen

⅔ C. sugar
⅔ C. light corn syrup
1 (16 oz.) jar crunchy
   peanut butter

3 C. corn flakes cereal
2 C. milk chocolate
   chips

In a heavy saucepan over medium heat, combine sugar and syrup until boiling. Add peanut butter. Mix until well blended. Remove from heat and stir in corn flake cereal, making sure to coat well. Press mixture into a greased 9 x 13″ pan. In a small saucepan over low heat, melt chocolate chips. Spread melted chocolate over ingredients in pan. Let chill for 20 to 25 minutes before cutting into bars.

Coconut Fudge Bars

Makes 32 servings

1 C. butter or margarine, melted, divided

14 graham crackers, finely crushed

1 C. sugar

1 (5 oz.) can evaporated milk

1 (10.5 oz.) pkg. miniature marshmallows

2 C. or 1 (12 oz.) pkg. chocolate chunks

1 C. chopped walnuts

1 C. shredded coconut, toasted*

In a medium bowl, combine ¾ cup melted butter and graham cracker crumbs. Press mixture onto bottom of a foil-lined 9 x 13" pan and set aside. In a large saucepan over medium heat, combine remaining ¼ cup melted butter, sugar, evaporated milk and marshmallows. Heat to a boil and let boil for 5 minutes, stirring constantly. Add chocolate and heat until completely melted, stirring constantly. Pour mixture immediately over crust and spread evenly. Sprinkle top with chopped walnuts and toasted coconut, pressing them lightly into the chocolate. Refrigerate for 2 hours before cutting into bars.

To toast, place coconut in a single layer on a baking sheet. Bake at 350° for 5 to 7 minutes, stirring occasionally, until coconut is golden brown.

Crispy Caramel Bars

Makes 2 dozen

3 T. butter or
   margarine
1 (10.5 oz.) pkg.
   miniature marshmallows

½ C. caramel topping
6 C. crispy rice cereal

In a large saucepan over low heat, melt butter. Add marshmallows and stir until completely melted. Remove from heat. Add caramel topping and stir until well combined. Add crispy rice cereal, stirring until completely coated. Using a greased spatula, press mixture evenly into a greased 9 x 13″ pan. Let cool before cutting into 2″ squares. Serve immediately.

Healthy Peanut Bars

Makes 1 dozen

1½ C. quick oats
½ C. honey
½ C. wheat germ

½ C. crunchy peanut
   butter
½ C. chopped
   peanuts

In a medium bowl, combine quick cooking oats, honey, wheat germ, crunchy peanut butter and chopped peanuts. Mix thoroughly, until well combined. Shape mixture into a long rectangle and wrap in waxed paper. Chill in refrigerator until hardened. Cut into 1″ thick bars and serve.

Cherry Coconut Bars

Makes 1 dozen

¼ C. butter or margarine

1 (10.5 oz.) pkg. miniature marshmallows

5 C. crispy rice cereal

1 C. shredded coconut

½ C. coarsely chopped peanuts, optional

½ C. chopped maraschino cherries

In a large saucepan over low heat, melt butter. Add marshmallows and stir until completely melted. Remove from heat. Add crispy rice cereal, coconut, peanuts and chopped cherries, stirring until completely coated. Using a greased spatula, press mixture evenly into a greased 9 x 9″ pan. Let cool in refrigerator for 30 minutes before cutting into bars.

Chocolate Yummies

Makes 1 dozen

7 graham crackers
2½ C. miniature
  marshmallows
1 (12 oz.) pkg.
  chocolate chips
⅔ C. light corn syrup

3 T. butter or
  margarine
½ C. crunchy peanut
  butter
3 C. crispy rice cereal

Grease a 9 x 13″ microwave-safe pan. Place 6 graham crackers in a single layer on the bottom of the pan. Cut remaining graham cracker to fit in remainder of bottom. Sprinkle marshmallows evenly over graham crackers. Microwave on high for 1 minute, until marshmallows are puffy. Remove from microwave and let cool completely. In a large microwave-safe mixing bowl, combine chocolate chips, corn syrup and butter. Microwave on high for 1½ minutes or until chocolate can be stirred smooth. Stir in peanut butter and add crispy rice cereal. Mix until well combined. Spread mixture evenly over marshmallows in pan. Cover and refrigerate for 1 hour, until firm. Cut into bars and store in an air-tight container in refrigerator.

Caramel Cashew Crunchies

Makes 1 dozen

1 (14 oz.) bag
caramels, wrappers
removed

2 T. butter or
margarine

6 C. cocoa crispy
rice cereal

1 C. cashews

1 C. white baking
chips, divided

In a large microwave-safe bowl, combine caramels, butter and 2 tablespoons water. Microwave on high for 3 minutes, stirring after each minute, until melted and smooth. Add cocoa crispy rice cereal and cashews. Stir until well coated. Add ½ cup white baking chips, stirring until well combined. Spread mixture into a greased 9 x 13″ pan. Let stand for 2 minutes. Sprinkle remaining ½ cup white baking chips over mixture and press evenly into pan. Let cool before cutting into 2″ squares.

Strawberry Margarita Bars

Makes 1 dozen

1¼ C. crushed
  pretzels
¼ C. butter or
  margarine, melted
1 (14 oz.) can sweetened
  condensed milk
1 C. pureed
  strawberries

½ C. lime juice
1 (8 oz.) container
  whipped topping
Fresh sliced
  strawberries for
  garnish, optional

In a 9 x 13″ pan, mix crushed pretzels and melted butter. Press crumb mixture firmly into the bottom of the pan and chill in refrigerator while preparing filling. In a large bowl, combine sweetened condensed milk, pureed strawberries and lime juice until well blended. Gently fold in whipped topping and pour mixture into chilled crust. Freeze 6 hours or overnight. Let stand at room temperature for 15 minutes before cutting to serve. If desired, garnish with fresh sliced strawberries.

Peanut Butter Cereal Bars

Makes 32 servings

1 (16 oz.) pkg. Honey Bunches of Oats cereal, any kind

1 C. sugar
1 C. light corn syrup
1 C. peanut butter

In a large bowl, place Honey Bunches of Oats cereal and set aside. In a medium microwave-safe bowl, combine sugar, corn syrup and peanut butter. Microwave on high for 4 to 5 minutes, until mixture begins to boil. Pour mixture over cereal and stir until well coated. Press mixture into a greased 9 x 13″ pan. Let cool before cutting into bars.

Nutty Caramel Squares

Makes 2 dozen

4 C. powdered sugar
1½ C. crushed graham crackers
1½ C. peanut butter
1½ C. chopped almonds, divided

¾ C. plus 3 T. butter or margarine, divided
48 caramels, wrappers removed
1 C. chocolate chunks

In a large bowl, combine powdered sugar, crushed graham crackers, peanut butter, 1 cup chopped almonds and ¾ cup melted butter. Mix well and press mixture into a greased 9 x 13″ pan. In a large saucepan over low heat, melt caramels in ¼ cup water, stirring frequently until mixture is melted and smooth. Pour over crust. In a separate large saucepan over low heat, melt chocolate and remaining 3 tablespoons butter, stirring often until melted and smooth. Spread mixture over caramel layer. Immediately sprinkle remaining ½ cup chopped almonds over all and gently press into topping. Refrigerate at least 1 hour before cutting into squares.

Peanut Butter Cracker Squares

Makes 25 servings

1 C. marshmallow creme

1 C. chunky peanut butter

36 Ritz crackers, finely crushed

½ C. miniature chocolate chips

1 (1 oz.) square semisweet chocolate, melted

In a medium bowl, combine marshmallow creme and peanut butter. Stir in crushed Ritz crackers and chocolate chips. Lightly press mixture into a greased 9 x 9″ baking pan. Drizzle with melted chocolate. Let stand at room temperature for 30 minutes, until set, before cutting into squares.

No-Bake Walnut Brownies

Makes 3 dozen

2½ C. finely crushed graham crackers

2 C. miniature marshmallows

1 C. chopped walnuts

1 C. chocolate chips

1 C. evaporated milk

½ C. light corn syrup

¼ tsp. salt

1 T. butter or margarine

1 T. vanilla

In a large bowl, combine crushed graham crackers, marshmallows and chopped walnuts. Set aside. In a 2-quart saucepan over low heat, combine chocolate chips, evaporated milk, corn syrup and salt. Heat to a rapid boil for 10 minutes, stirring constantly. Remove from heat and stir in butter and vanilla. Immediately stir chocolate mixture into crumb mixture. Spread all into a greased 9 x 9″ pan. Refrigerate for approximately 3 hours, until set, before cutting into squares.

Crispy Kiss Squares

Makes 2 dozen

6 C. Cocoa Puffs
  cereal
¼ C. butter or
  margarine
40 large
  marshmallows

1 (11.5 oz.) pkg.
  chocolate chips
24 striped chocolate
  kisses

In a large bowl, place Cocoa Puffs cereal and set aside. In a microwave-safe bowl, combine butter and marshmallows. Microwave on high for 3 minutes. Stir and continue heating, as needed, until smooth, stirring after every minute. Add chocolate chips and mix until chocolate chips are completely melted. Pour melted mixture over cereal in bowl. Spread mixture evenly into a 9 x 13″ baking dish. Place striped chocolate kisses in rows over the top. Let cool completely before cutting into squares.

Chewy Chocolate Cherry Bars

Makes 16 servings

1½ C. crushed Oreo
cookies, divided
2 T. butter or
margarine, melted
1 C. boiling water
2 (6 oz.) pkgs. cherry
gelatin

⅔ C. chopped
maraschino
cherries
½ C. light corn syrup
2 C. whipped topping

In a medium bowl, combine 1 cup crushed Oreo cookies and melted butter. Press mixture firmly into bottom of a greased 9 x 9″ pan. In a medium bowl, combine boiling water and cherry gelatin. Stir at least 2 minutes, until completely dissolved. Add chopped cherries and corn syrup, stirring until well blended. Refrigerate 30 minutes, until slightly thickened. Pour mixture over crust. Refrigerate for an additional 3 hours until firm. Before serving, spread whipped topping over bars and sprinkle with remaining ½ cup crushed Oreo cookies. Cut into squares before serving.

Chocolate Covered Crunch Bars

Makes 8 servings

32 large marshmallows
¼ C. butter or margarine

½ tsp. vanilla
5 C. corn flakes cereal
1 C. chocolate chips

Grease a 9 x 9″ pan and set aside. In a large saucepan over low heat, melt marshmallows and butter, stirring constantly, until mixture is smooth. Remove from heat and stir in vanilla. Stir in half of the cornflakes at a time until evenly coated. Press mixture into prepared pan. In a small saucepan over low heat or a double boiler, heat chocolate chips, stirring frequently, until melted. Spread melted chocolate over corn flake mixture in pan. Let cool before cutting into 2″ bars.

Chocolate Caramel & Nut Treats

Makes 4 dozen

12 graham crackers   **1 C. chocolate chips**
¾ C. brown sugar   **1 C. salted peanuts**
¾ C. butter

Line a 10 x 15″ jellyroll pan with graham crackers. In a large saucepan over medium heat, combine brown sugar and butter. Cook until mixture comes to a full boil. Boil for 5 minutes, stirring constantly. Immediately pour over graham crackers in pan and spread evenly. Sprinkle with chocolate chips and let stand for 1 minute. Sprinkle with peanuts and lightly press into chocolate. Let cool completely before cutting or breaking into squares.

Orange Chocolate Cream Squares

Makes 2 dozen

1¼ C. finely crushed chocolate wafer cookies

⅔ C. plus 1 T. butter, melted, divided

1½ C. powdered sugar

2 tsp. grated orange peel

1 T. milk

½ tsp. vanilla

1 T. cocoa powder

In a medium bowl, combine crushed chocolate wafer cookies and ⅓ cup melted butter. Press mixture onto the bottom of a greased 8 x 8″ or 9 x 9″ pan. Cover and refrigerate for 1 hour, until firm. In a medium mixing bowl, combine powdered sugar, ⅓ cup melted butter, grated orange peel, milk and vanilla. Beat at medium speed for 3 to 4 minutes, until creamy. Spread mixture over cooled crust. In a separate small bowl, combine remaining 1 tablespoon melted butter and cocoa powder. Drizzle over ingredients in pan. Refrigerate for 1 to 2 hours, until firm, before cutting into bars.

Caramel Candy Crunch Squares

Makes 3 dozen

4 C. corn Chex cereal
1 C. salted peanuts
1 C. M&M candies
½ C. butter

1 C. brown sugar
½ C. light corn syrup
2 T. flour

In a large bowl, combine cereal, peanuts and M&Ms and set aside. In a large saucepan over low heat, melt butter. Stir in brown sugar, corn syrup and flour. Increase heat to medium and cook mixture, stirring occasionally, until mixture comes to a full boil. Boil for 1 minute and pour over cereal in bowl. Stir until well coated and press into the bottom of a greased 9 x 13″ pan. Let cool completely before cutting into bars.

Mocha Bars

Makes 18 servings

15 chocolate graham
  crackers, divided
2 (8 oz.) pkgs. cream
  cheese, softened
3½ C. milk, divided
3 (6 oz.) pkgs. instant
  chocolate pudding
  mix

1 T. instant coffee
¼ tsp. cinnamon
1 (8 oz.) container
  whipped topping,
  divided
1 (1 oz.) square
  semisweet
  chocolate, grated

Place half of the chocolate graham crackers onto the bottom of a greased 9 x 13″ pan, cutting crackers to fit, if necessary. In a large mixing bowl, beat softened cream cheese at low speed until smooth. Gradually beat in 1 cup milk. Add remaining milk, chocolate pudding mixes, instant coffee and cinnamon. Beat 1 to 2 minutes, until mixture thickens. Gently stir in 2 cups whipped topping. Spread half of the pudding mixture over graham crackers in pan. Arrange remaining half of graham crackers over pudding layer. Top with remaining pudding mixture and cover with remaining whipped topping. Sprinkle with grated chocolate. Freeze for 3 hours or overnight before cutting into bars.

Fudgy Nut Bars

Makes 2 dozen

1 C. butter or
  margarine, divided
1 C. chocolate chips,
  divided
1¾ C. crushed
  graham crackers
1 C. shredded
  coconut

½ C. chopped nuts
1 (8 oz.) pkg. cream
  cheese, softened
½ C. sugar
1 tsp. vanilla

In a large saucepan over low heat, melt ¾ cup butter and ⅓ cup chocolate chips, stirring until smooth. In a medium bowl, combine crushed graham crackers, coconut and chopped nuts. Stir into butter mixture in saucepan. Mix well and press mixture onto the bottom of an ungreased 10 x 15″ jellyroll pan. Refrigerate for 30 minutes, until firm. In a medium mixing bowl, beat softened cream cheese, sugar and vanilla at medium speed until well blended. Spread mixture over crust. Refrigerate for an additional 30 minutes, until firm. In a separate saucepan over low heat or double boiler, melt remaining ¼ cup butter and remaining ⅔ cup chocolate chips. Once melted, spread mixture over cream cheese layer in pan. Refrigerate until firm before cutting into squares.

Yummy Granola Snack Squares

Makes 18 servings

2½ C. crispy rice cereal
2 C. quick oats
½ C. raisins
½ C. brown sugar

½ C. light corn syrup
½ C. crunchy peanut butter
1 tsp. vanilla

In a large bowl, combine crispy rice cereal, oats and raisins. Mix well and set aside. In a small saucepan over medium heat, combine brown sugar and corn syrup. Bring to a boil, remove from heat and stir in peanut butter and vanilla. Pour mixture over cereal mixture and toss until evenly coated. Press mixture into a greased 9 x 13″ baking dish and spread evenly. Let cool to room temperature before cutting into squares.

White Christmas

Makes 1 dozen

3 C. crispy rice cereal
1 C. shredded coconut
¾ C. evaporated milk
½ C. powdered sugar
2 oz. mixed candied fruit, chopped
2 oz. red and green candied cherries, chopped
¼ C. raisins
4½ oz. shortening, cut into pieces
4½ oz. white chocolate baking chips

Generously grease a 9 x 13″ baking dish and set aside. In a large bowl, combine crispy rice cereal, coconut, evaporated milk, powdered sugar, chopped candied fruit, chopped candied cherries and raisins. In a double boiler, combine shortening and white chocolate baking chips. Heat over simmering water until mixture is melted and smooth. Pour white chocolate mixture over crispy rice mixture and mix well. Press all into prepared pan. Chill in refrigerator until set. Let stand for 10 minutes before cutting into bars.

Chocolate Peanut Butter Squares

Makes 1 dozen

¾ C. margarine, melted

1½ C. peanut butter

1 lb. powdered sugar

1 (12 oz.) pkg. chocolate chips

In a large bowl, combine melted margarine, peanut butter and powdered sugar. Press mixture into the bottom of a greased 9 x 13″ pan. In a double boiler, melt chocolate chips. Spread melted chocolate evenly over ingredients in pan. Let cool before cutting into 1″ squares.

Cherry Crunch Bars

Makes 2 dozen

3 T. butter or
    margarine
1 (10.5 oz.) pkg.
    miniature
    marshmallows
2 tsp. cherry extract

1 tsp. red food
    coloring, optional
6 C. crispy rice cereal
½ C. dried tart
    cherries

In a large saucepan over low heat, melt butter. Add marshmallows and stir until completely melted. Remove from heat. Stir in cherry extract and red food coloring. Add crispy rice cereal and dried cherries, stirring until completely coated. Using a greased spatula, press mixture evenly into a greased 9 x 13″ pan. Let cool before cutting into 2″ squares. Serve immediately.

Caramel Crispy Treats

Makes 32 servings

4 (2.05 oz.) Milky
  Way bars
¾ C. butter or
  margarine, divided

3 C. crispy rice cereal
1 C. milk chocolate
  chips

In microwave or a double boiler, melt candy bars and ½ cup butter, stirring occasionally, until smooth. Stir in cereal until well coated. Press mixture into a greased 7 x 11″ pan. In a separate microwave-safe bowl or double boiler, melt chocolate chips and remaining ¼ cup butter, stirring until smooth. Remove from heat and spread chocolate mixture over ingredients in pan. Refrigerate 1 hour, or until firm, before cutting into squares.

NO BAKE PIES

Chocolate Mocha Pie

Makes 1 (9″) pie

1 (3.4 oz.) pkg. cook & serve chocolate pudding mix

2½ C. milk, divided

2 tsp. instant coffee granules

2 T. sugar

1 (9") prepared chocolate cookie crumb crust

1 (1.3 oz.) env. whipped topping mix

½ tsp. vanilla

1 (1.75 oz.) pkg. chocolate sprinkles, optional

Prepare chocolate pudding mix according to package directions using 2 cups of the milk. In a small bowl, combine 1 cup prepared chocolate pudding, instant coffee granules and sugar. Stir until sugar is dissolved and chill in refrigerator. Let remaining prepared chocolate pudding chill for 5 minutes, stirring occasionally. Pour chilled chocolate pudding into prepared crust. Chill in refrigerator. Meanwhile, prepare whipped topping mix according to package directions using the remaining ½ cup milk and vanilla. Remove the reserved pudding and coffee mixture from the refrigerator and beat well. Blend mixture into whipped topping. Pile topping lightly over pudding in crust, making sure to spread evenly. Chill pie several hours before serving. If desired, top with chocolate sprinkles. Store in refrigerator.

Double Layer Chocolate Peanut Butter Pie

Makes 1 (9″) pie

½ (8 oz.) pkg. cream
  cheese, softened
1 T. sugar
2 C. plus 1 T. milk,
  divided
1 C. peanut butter
1 (8 oz.) container
  whipped topping,
  divided

1 (9″) prepared
  graham cracker
  crust
2 (3.9 oz.) pkgs.
  instant chocolate
  pudding mix
4 peanut butter cups,
  cut into ½″ pieces

In a large bowl, combine softened cream cheese, sugar, 1 tablespoon milk and peanut butter until smooth. Gently stir in 1½ cups whipped topping. Spread mixture evenly over the bottom of the prepared pie crust. In a separate bowl, combine chocolate pudding mixes with remaining 2 cups milk. Mix well until thick. Immediately fold in remaining whipped topping. Spread mixture evenly over layer in pie crust. Scatter peanut butter cup pieces over top of pie. Cover and refrigerate for 4 hours before serving. Store in refrigerator.

Quick and Easy Lemon Pie

Makes 1 (9") pie

1 (3.4 oz.) pkg. cook
   & serve lemon
   pudding mix
1 (8 oz.) pkg. cream
   cheese, softened
½ (14 oz.) can
   sweetened
   condensed milk

3 T. lemon juice
1 (9") prepared
   graham cracker
   crust
1 (8 oz.) container
   whipped topping

Prepare lemon pudding according to package directions in a large saucepan. When pudding thickens, reduce heat to low. Stir in softened cream cheese, sweetened condensed milk and lemon juice, making sure to stir frequently as mixture may stick to saucepan. Pour mixture into prepared pie crust. Cover and chill in refrigerator. Before serving, spread whipped topping evenly over pie. Store in refrigerator.

Fluffy Lemon Fruit Pie

Makes 1 (9") pie

1 (21 oz.) can cherry
  pie filling, divided
1 (9") prepared
  graham cracker
  crust
1 (8 oz.) pkg. cream
  cheese, softened

1 C. milk
1 (3.4 oz.) pkg.
  instant lemon
  pudding mix
1 (8 oz.) container
  whipped topping,
  divided

Spread half of the cherry filling evenly over bottom of prepared pie crust. In a large bowl, beat softened cream cheese with a wire whisk until smooth. Gradually beat in milk until well blended. Add lemon pudding mix and beat until smooth. Gently fold in half of the whipped topping. Spread cream cheese and lemon pudding mixture evenly over cherry filling in pie crust. Spread remaining whipped topping over cream cheese and lemon pudding layer. Top with remaining cherry pie filling. Cover and chill in refrigerator 3 hours before serving. Store in refrigerator.

Frozen Peanut Butter Cheesecake

Makes 1 (9″) pie

⅓ C. butter
1 C. chocolate chips
1¾ C. crispy rice cereal
1 (8 oz.) pkg. cream cheese, softened
1¼ C. sweetened condensed milk

¾ C. peanut butter
2 T. lemon juice
1 tsp. vanilla
1 C. whipped topping
½ C. chocolate fudge sauce

In a heavy saucepan, melt butter and chocolate chips over low heat. Remove from heat and gently stir in crispy rice cereal until evenly coated. Press mixture into the bottom and up sides of a 9″ pie pan. Chill in refrigerator for 30 minutes. In a large bowl, beat softened cream cheese with a wire whisk until smooth and fluffy. Gradually beat in sweetened condensed milk and peanut butter. Mix well until smooth. Stir in lemon juice and vanilla and fold in whipped topping. Pour mixture into prepared crust. Drizzle chocolate fudge sauce over pie and freeze for 4 hours or until firm. Store in freezer until ready to serve.

Chocolate Mint Pie

Makes 1 (9") pie

2½ C. crushed Oreo
  cookies, divided
¼ C. butter, melted
1 qt. mint chocolate
  chip ice cream,
  softened, divided
4 T. plus 2 tsp. crème
  de menthe liqueur,
  divided

3 egg whites
Salt to taste
¼ tsp. cream
  of tartar
⅓ C. sugar

In a large bowl, combine 1½ cups crushed Oreo cookies and melted butter. Press mixture firmly over bottom and up sides of a 9″ pie pan. Freeze for 1 to 2 hours. Spread half of softened mint chocolate chip ice cream into prepared crust. Drizzle 2 tablespoons crème de menthe liqueur evenly over ice cream and sprinkle ½ cup crushed Oreo cookies over ice cream. Repeat layers with remaining ice cream, 2 tablespoons crème de menthe and remaining ½ cup crushed Oreo cookies. In a medium mixing bowl, beat egg whites until foamy. Add salt and cream of tartar and beat until mixture is slightly stiff. Gradually beat in sugar until soft peaks form. Fold in remaining 2 teaspoons crème de menthe liqueur. Spread mixture evenly over pie. Freeze up to 24 hours. Just before serving, place pie in broiler until top is golden. Store in freezer.

Frosty Pumpkin Pie

Makes 1 (9″) pie

1 C. pumpkin puree
½ C. brown sugar
½ tsp. salt
½ tsp. cinnamon
½ tsp. ginger
¼ tsp. nutmeg
1 qt. vanilla ice
   cream, softened

1 (9″) pre-baked
   pie crust
Whipped topping
   and walnut halves
   for garnish,
   optional

In a large bowl, combine pumpkin puree, brown sugar, salt, cinnamon, ginger and nutmeg with a hand mixer. Blend in vanilla ice cream. Pour mixture into baked pie crust and freeze until firm. Serve pie frozen. If desired, garnish with whipped topping and walnut halves. Store in freezer.

Black Forest Pie

Makes 1 (9") pie

4 (1 oz.) squares
  unsweetened
  chocolate, broken
  into pieces
1 (14 oz.) can sweetened
  condensed milk
1 tsp. almond extract
1½ C. heavy
  whipping cream

1 (9") pre-baked
  pie crust
1 (21 oz.) can cherry
  pie filling, chilled
⅛ C. sliced
  almonds, toasted,
  optional*

In a heavy saucepan, combine unsweetened chocolate and sweetened condensed milk. Cook, over medium heat, stirring constantly, until chocolate is melted. Remove from heat and stir in almond extract. Pour mixture into a large bowl and chill in refrigerator. When chilled thoroughly, remove mixture from refrigerator and beat until smooth. In a separate bowl, beat heavy cream until stiff. Gradually fold in chocolate mixture. Pour all into baked pie crust. Refrigerate 4 to 6 hours, until set. Just before serving, top with cherry filling. If desired, garnish with toasted almonds. Store leftovers in refrigerator.

To toast, place almonds in a single layer on a baking sheet. Bake at 350° for approximately 10 minutes or until almonds are golden brown.

Chocolate Supreme Pie

Makes 1 (9″) pie

25 large
  marshmallows
5 (1.5 oz.) milk
  chocolate bars
½ C. milk

1 (8 oz.) container
  whipped topping
1 (9″) prepared
  graham cracker
  crust

In a medium saucepan over low heat, combine marshmallows, chocolate bars and milk. Cook, stirring frequently, until marshmallows and chocolate are melted and mixture is smooth. Remove from heat and let cool for 30 minutes. Fold whipped topping into chocolate mixture and pour all into prepared pie crust. Chill in refrigerator for 24 hours before serving. Store in freezer.

Fresh Blueberry Pie

Makes 1 (8″) pie

4 C. fresh blueberries,
   divided
1 (8″) pre-baked pie
   crust, cooled
1 T. flour

1 T. butter
1 T. lemon juice
½ C. sugar
Whipped topping,
   optional

Pour 2 cups blueberries into prepared and cooled pie crust. In a medium saucepan, combine flour, butter, lemon juice and sugar. Mix well. Add remaining 2 cups blueberries. Bring mixture just to a boil over medium heat, until berries begin to pop open. Pour cooked berries over fresh berries in pie crust. Chill pie in refrigerator until ready to serve. If desired, serve with whipped topping. Store at room temperature or in refrigerator.

Peanut Butter Cream Pie

Makes 1 (9") pie

½ (8 oz.) pkg. cream cheese, softened
1 C. powdered sugar
⅓ C. creamy peanut butter
1 C. whipped topping

1 (9") prepared graham cracker crust
¼ C. finely chopped peanuts

In a large bowl, beat softened cream cheese with a wire whisk until soft and fluffy. Add powdered sugar and peanut butter and beat well. Fold in whipped topping. Pour filling into prepared pie crust. Sprinkle chopped peanuts over top. Chill in refrigerator until firm. Store in refrigerator.

Pumpkin Ice Cream Pie

Makes 1 (9") pie

1½ C. crushed
graham crackers
¼ C. butter or
margarine, melted
3 T. sugar
½ gal. vanilla ice
cream, softened

1 C. canned pumpkin
½ C. brown sugar
1 tsp. ginger
½ tsp. cinnamon
½ tsp. nutmeg
1 T. orange juice

In a large bowl, combine crushed graham crackers, melted butter and sugar. Mix well. Firmly press mixture into an 8" or 9" pie pan. Chill pie crust for 1 hour. In a separate bowl, combine vanilla ice cream, canned pumpkin, brown sugar, ginger, cinnamon, nutmeg and orange juice. Pour mixture into cooled pie crust. Freeze until ready to serve. Store in freezer.

Lemonade Pie

Makes 1 (9″) pie

½ (12 oz.) can frozen lemonade concentrate, thawed

1 (14 oz.) can sweetened condensed milk

1 (8 oz.) container whipped topping

1 (9″) prepared graham cracker crust

In a large bowl, combine thawed lemonade concentrate and sweetened condensed milk. Fold in whipped topping. Pour filling evenly into crust. Chill in refrigerator until ready to serve. Store in refrigerator or freezer.

Margarita Party Pie

Makes 1 (9″) pie

1½ C. crushed pretzels

¼ C. sugar

⅔ C. butter, melted

1 (14 oz.) can sweetened condensed milk

¼ C. fresh lime juice

¼ C. tequila

4 T. orange liqueur

1 C. sliced fresh or frozen strawberries

2 drops red food coloring

2 drops yellow food coloring

2 C. whipped topping, divided

In a large bowl, combine crushed pretzels, sugar and butter. Mix well and firmly press mixture into bottom of a 9″ pie pan. In a separate bowl, combine sweetened condensed milk, lime juice, tequila and orange liqueur. Pour half of the mixture into another bowl. Add strawberries and red food coloring to one bowl. Add yellow food coloring to the other bowl. Fold 1 cup whipped topping into each bowl. Spoon filling into prepared crust, alternating colors. Freeze for 4 hours or overnight. Store in freezer.

Pumpkin Pie

Makes 1 (9″) pie

1 (¼ oz.) pkg.
  unflavored gelatin
1 tsp. cinnamon
½ tsp. ginger
½ tsp. nutmeg
½ tsp. salt
1 (14 oz.) can
  sweetened
  condensed milk

2 eggs, beaten
1 (15 oz.) can
  pumpkin puree
1 (9″) prepared
  graham cracker
  crust

In a heavy saucepan, combine gelatin, cinnamon, ginger, nutmeg and salt. Stir in sweetened condensed milk and beaten eggs. Mix well and let stand for 1 minute. Place on burner over low heat, stirring constantly, for about 10 minutes, until gelatin dissolves and mixture thickens. Remove from heat. Stir in pumpkin, mixing thoroughly, and pour mixture into prepared pie crust. Chill in refrigerator at least 3 hours before serving. Store in refrigerator.

Old-Fashioned Coconut Cream Pie

Makes 1 (9″) pie

3 C. half n' half
2 eggs
¾ C. sugar
½ C. flour
¼ tsp. salt
1 C. shredded coconut,
  toasted, divided*

1 tsp. vanilla
1 (9″) pre-baked
  pie crust
1 C. whipped topping

In a medium saucepan, combine half n' half, eggs, sugar, flour and salt. Bring mixture to a boil over low heat, stirring constantly. Remove from heat and stir in ¾ cup shredded coconut and vanilla. Pour in prepared pie crust and chill in refrigerator for 2 to 4 hours, until firm. Top evenly with whipped topping and remaining ¼ cup shredded coconut. Store in refrigerator.

*To toast, place coconut in a single layer on a baking sheet. Bake at 350° for 5 to 7 minutes, stirring occasionally, until coconut is golden brown.

Toasted Coconut Pecan Caramel Pie

Makes 2 (9″) pies

¼ C. butter
1 (7 oz.) pkg. shredded coconut
½ C. chopped pecans
1 (8 oz.) pkg. cream cheese, softened
1 (14 oz.) can sweetened condensed milk

1 (12 oz.) container whipped topping
2 (9″) pre-baked pie crusts
1 (12 oz.) jar caramel topping, divided

In a medium saucepan over medium heat, melt butter. Add shredded coconut and chopped pecans. Toss well and sauté until coconut is lightly browned. Set aside to cool. In a large mixing bowl, beat softened cream cheese with a wire whisk until fluffy. Add sweetened condensed milk and mix until smooth. Fold in whipped topping. Spread ¼ of cream cheese mixture into each prepared pie crust. Sprinkle ¼ of coconut mixture over cream cheese mixture in each pie. Drizzle half of caramel topping over coconut in each pie crust. Repeat layers with remaining cream cheese mixture and remaining coconut mixture. Pies may be served chilled or frozen. Store in refrigerator or freezer.

Key Lime Pie

Makes 1 (10″) pie

1 T. grated lime peel
1 C. fresh lime juice
1 (14 oz.) can
   sweetened
   condensed milk
1 (3.4 oz.) pkg.
   instant vanilla
   pudding mix

1 (8 oz.) container
   whipped topping
1 (10″) prepared
   graham cracker
   crust

In a large bowl, combine lime peel, lime juice and sweetened condensed milk. Whisk in vanilla pudding mix and allow to set for 5 minutes. Fold in whipped topping. Pour mixture into prepared pie crust. Chill in refrigerator at least 2 hours before serving. If desired, garnish with additional whipped topping. Store in refrigerator or freezer.

Hawaiian Millionaire Pie

Makes 1 (9″) pie

1 (15 oz.) can crushed
  pineapple, drained
¼ C. lemon juice
1 (12 oz.) container
  whipped topping
½ C. chopped
  maraschino
  cherries

1 (14 oz.) can
  sweetened
  condensed milk
1 C. chopped walnuts
  or pecans
1 (9″) prepared
  graham cracker
  crust

In a large bowl, combine crushed pineapple, lemon juice, whipped topping, chopped cherries, sweetened condensed milk and chopped nuts. Mix well. Pour mixture into prepared pie crust. Chill in refrigerator at least 1 hour before serving. Store in refrigerator or freezer.

Fresh Strawberry Pie

Makes 2 (9″) pies

1 C. sugar
2 T. cornstarch
1 C. boiling water
1 (3 oz.) pkg. strawberry flavored gelatin
2½ qts. fresh strawberries, quartered

2 (9″) prepared graham cracker crusts
Whipped topping, optional

In a large saucepan, combine sugar and cornstarch. Mix well to completely blend in cornstarch. Add boiling water and cook over medium heat until mixture thickens. Remove from heat and add strawberry gelatin. Stir until smooth. Let mixture cool to room temperature. Place quartered strawberries in prepared pie crusts. Pour cooled gelatin mixture over strawberries. Refrigerate until set. If desired, serve with whipped topping. Store in refrigerator or freezer.

French Peach Pie

Makes 1 (9″) pie

1 (15 oz.) can sliced
  peaches in juice
1 (3.4 oz.) pkg.
  instant vanilla
  pudding mix
1 C. milk
1 C. sour cream

¼ tsp. almond extract
1 (9") prepared
  graham cracker
  crust
1 T. cornstarch
1 tsp. lemon juice

Drain peaches, reserving ⅔ cup juice. In a large bowl, combine vanilla pudding mix, milk, sour cream and almond extract. Stir for 2 minutes, until smooth. Pour filling into prepared pie crust. Chill for 10 minutes. Arrange peach slices in an even pattern over filling in pie crust. In a small saucepan, combine reserved peach juice and cornstarch over low medium heat. Bring to a boil for 2 minutes. Remove from heat and stir in lemon juice. Pour glaze over peaches in pie. Chill in refrigerator until set. Store in refrigerator.

Double Layer Pumpkin Pie

Makes 1 (9″) pie

½ (8 oz.) pkg. cream cheese, softened
1 C. plus 1 T. milk, divided
1 T. sugar
1½ C. whipped topping
1 (9″) prepared graham cracker crust, chilled

2 (3.4 oz.) pkgs. instant vanilla pudding mix
1 (15 oz.) can pumpkin puree
1 tsp. cinnamon
½ tsp. ground ginger
¼ tsp. ground cloves

In a large bowl, whisk together softened cream cheese, 1 tablespoon milk and sugar until smooth. Gently fold in whipped topping. Spread mixture over bottom of prepared chilled pie crust. Let set in refrigerator for 1 hour. In a separate bowl, combine remaining 1 cup milk, vanilla pudding mix, pumpkin, cinnamon, ginger and ground cloves. Mix well until thickened. Spread mixture over cream cheese layer in pie crust. Refrigerate for 4 hours, until set. Store in refrigerator.

Creamy Lemon Pie

Makes 1 (9") pie

⅔ C. fresh lemon juice

1 (14 oz.) can sweetened condensed milk

1 (12 oz.) container whipped topping

1 (9") prepared graham cracker crust

In a medium bowl, combine fresh lemon juice, sweetened condensed milk and whipped topping. Mix well and pour mixture into prepared pie crust. Chill in refrigerator for 2 hours before serving. Store in refrigerator.

Coconut Cream Pie

Makes 1 (9″) pie

1 (3.4 oz.) pkg.
  instant coconut
  pudding mix
1½ C. milk
1 C. shredded
  coconut
1 (8 oz.) container
  whipped topping,
  divided

1 (9″) pre-baked pie
  crust
½ C. shredded
  coconut, toasted*

In a large bowl, combine coconut pudding mix and milk. Mix well until pudding thickens. Fold in shredded coconut and half of the whipped topping. Pour mixture into prepared pie crust. Spread remaining half of whipped topping evenly over mixture in pie. Sprinkle with toasted shredded coconut. Chill in refrigerator for 1 hour before serving. Store in refrigerator.

To toast, place coconut in a single layer on a baking sheet. Bake at 350° for 5 to 7 minutes, stirring occasionally, until coconut is golden brown.

Chocolate Peanut Butter Pie

Makes 1 (9″) pie

2 (4 oz.) pkgs. single
  serving chocolate
  pudding cups
⅓ C. creamy peanut
  butter

1 (8 oz.) container
  whipped topping
1 (9″) prepared graham
  cracker crust

In a large bowl, combine chocolate pudding and peanut butter. Stir until smooth. Fold in whipped topping and stir until completely blended. Pour filling into prepared pie crust. Freeze until firm. Let thaw in refrigerator 2 hours before serving. Store in refrigerator.

Easy Pineapple Pie

Makes 1 (9″) pie

1 (8 oz.) pkg. cream
  cheese, softened
¼ C. sugar
1 C. heavy whipping
  cream

1 (20 oz.) can crushed
  pineapple, drained
1 (9″) prepared graham
  cracker crust

In a large mixing bowl, beat together cream cheese and sugar, until light and fluffy. In a separate mixing bowl, beat heavy cream at high speed until soft peaks form. Fold whipped cream into cream cheese mixture. Carefully fold in drained pineapple. Pour filling into prepared pie crust. Chill in refrigerator for 2 to 3 hours, until filling has set.

Chocolate Mousse Pie

Makes 1 (9″) pie

1 tsp. unflavored gelatin
1 C. chocolate chips
¼ C. plus 2 T. sugar, divided
1 T. instant coffee granules
3 eggs, separated

1½ tsp. vanilla, divided
1½ C. heavy whipping cream, divided
1 (9″) pre-baked pie crust
2 T. cocoa powder
2 T. powdered sugar
½ tsp. almond extract

In a small bowl, combine 2 tablespoons water and unflavored gelatin and set aside. In a small saucepan, combine chocolate chips, ¼ cup sugar, instant coffee granules and 4 tablespoons water. Cook, stirring constantly, over low heat until chocolate is melted. Add gelatin mixture to saucepan and heat until dissolved. Remove from heat and beat in egg yolks. Return to heat and cook, stirring constantly, until mixture thickens slightly. Remove from heat and stir in 1 teaspoon vanilla. Let cool and set aside. Meanwhile, beat egg whites to soft peaks in a medium bowl. Gradually add remaining 2 tablespoons sugar and beat until stiff. Fold whipped mixture into chocolate mixture. In a separate bowl, whip ½ cup heavy cream until stiff. Fold whipped cream into chocolate mixture. Spoon mixture into pie crust. Chill in refrigerator. To make topping, in a large bowl, combine cocoa powder, powdered sugar and remaining 1 cup heavy cream. Let mixture chill for 30 minutes then whip until stiff peaks form. Stir in almond extract and remaining ½ teaspoon vanilla. Spread mixture evenly over filling in pie crust. Chill overnight until set. Store in refrigerator.

Chocolate Banana Cream Pie

Makes 1 (9″) pie

2 (1 oz.) squares
  semisweet chocolate

1½ C. plus 1 T. milk,
  divided

1 T. butter

1 (9″) pre-baked deep
  dish pie crust, cooled

2 bananas, peeled
  and sliced

1 (3.4 oz.) pkg. instant
  vanilla pudding mix

1½ C. shredded
  coconut

1½ C. whipped topping

2 T. shredded coconut,
  toasted*

In a medium microwave-safe bowl, combine chocolate squares, 1 tablespoon milk and butter. Microwave on high for 1 to 1½ minutes, stirring after every 30 seconds. Stir until chocolate is completely melted and spread evenly over prepared pie crust. Arrange banana slices over chocolate layer. In a large bowl, combine remaining 1½ cups milk and vanilla pudding mix. Beat with a wire whisk for 2 minutes. Stir in 1½ cups shredded coconut. Spoon mixture over bananas in pie crust. Spread whipped topping evenly over pie. Sprinkle toasted shredded coconut over whipped topping. Chill in refrigerator 4 hours, until set. Store in refrigerator.

To toast, place coconut in a single layer on a baking sheet. Bake at 350° for 5 to 7 minutes, stirring occasionally, until coconut is golden brown.

Chocolate Bar Pie

Makes 1 (9″) pie

6 (1.45 oz.) milk
  chocolate bars with
  almonds, broken
  into pieces
18 large
  marshmallows
½ C. milk

1 C. heavy whipping
  cream
1 tsp. vanilla
1 (9″) prepared
  graham cracker
  crust

In a medium saucepan, combine chocolate bar pieces, marshmallows and milk over medium heat. Cook, stirring frequently, until chocolate and marshmallows are melted and mixture is smooth. Remove from heat and let cool. In a medium bowl, whip heavy cream until soft peaks form. Fold into cooled chocolate mixture. Add vanilla and stir gently. Pour mixture into prepared pie crust. Chill in refrigerator 1 hour before serving. Store in refrigerator.

Chocolate Hazelnut Mocha Cappuccino Pie

Makes 1 (9") pie

1 (3.4 oz.) pkg. instant white chocolate pudding mix

1½ C. milk

2 T. instant mocha cappuccino mix

2 C. whipped topping, divided

1 (9") prepared chocolate cookie crumb crust

½ C. miniature chocolate chips, divided

½ C. chopped hazelnuts, divided

Prepare white chocolate pudding according to package directions using the 1½ cups milk and 2 tablespoons instant mocha cappuccino mix. Fold in ½ cup whipped topping. Spread mixture evenly into prepared pie crust. Sprinkle ¼ cup chocolate chips and ¼ cup chopped hazelnuts over pie. Cover and refrigerate for 2 hours. Before serving, spread remaining 1½ cups whipped topping over pie and sprinkle remaining ¼ cup chocolate chips and remaining ¼ cup chopped hazelnuts over whipped topping. Store in refrigerator.

Black Bing Cherry Pie

Makes 1 (9″) pie

1 (14 oz.) can
   sweetened
   condensed milk
Juice of 2 lemons
1 C. chopped pecans
1 (16.5 oz.) can pitted
   Bing cherries,
   drained

1 C. heavy whipping
   cream
1 (9″) prepared
   graham cracker
   crust

In a large bowl, combine sweetened condensed milk, lemon juice, chopped pecans and cherries. In a separate bowl, whip heavy cream into soft peaks. Fold whipped cream into cherry mixture. Pour all into prepared pie crust. Chill in refrigerator at least 4 hours before serving. Store in refrigerator.

Cherry Cheese Pie

Makes 1 (9″) pie

1 (8 oz.) pkg. cream
  cheese, softened
½ C. sugar
2 C. whipped topping

1 (9″) prepared graham
  cracker crust
1 (21 oz.) can cherry
  pie filling

In a medium mixing bowl, beat softened cream cheese and sugar with a wire whisk until light and fluffy. Fold in whipped topping and blend until mixture is smooth. Spread mixture evenly into prepared pie crust. Spoon cherry filling over mixture in pie crust. Cover with plastic wrap and chill in refrigerator 2 hours before serving. Store in refrigerator.

Caramel & Banana Pie

Makes 1 (9″) pie

2 (14 oz.) cans sweetened
  condensed milk
1 to 2 bananas, sliced

1 (9″) prepared pie crust
1 (12 oz.) container
  whipped topping

Remove paper from outside of sweetened condensed milk cans. Place unopened cans in a deep pan and add enough water to cover cans. Place over medium heat and bring to a boil. Let boil for 3 hours, adding more water as needed to keep water level over cans. After 1½ hours, carefully turn cans over. Remove cans from water and let cool. Place banana slices evenly in bottom of prepared pie crust. Carefully open cans and spoon caramelized mixture over bananas. Spoon whipped topping over banana mixture and serve. Store leftovers in refrigerator.

Banana Split Ice Cream Pie

Makes 1 (9") pie

2 bananas, peeled and sliced

1 (9") prepared chocolate cookie crumb crust

1 qt. strawberry ice cream, softened

1 (20 oz.) can crushed pineapple, drained

1 C. heavy whipping cream

¼ C. chopped walnuts

¼ C. maraschino cherries, optional

Arrange sliced bananas evenly over bottom of prepared pie crust. Spread softened strawberry ice cream in an even layer over bananas. Spread crushed pineapple over ice cream. In a medium bowl, whip heavy cream into soft peaks. Spread whipped cream over pineapple. Sprinkle chopped walnuts over whipped cream. Freeze pie for 3 hours, until slightly firm. If desired, garnish with cherries before serving. Store in freezer.

Banana Cream Pie

Makes 1 (9") pie

3 bananas, peeled and
   sliced, divided
1 (9") pre-baked pie
   crust, cooled
2½ C. milk
1 (3.4 oz.) pkg.
   instant French
   vanilla pudding
   mix

1 (3.4 oz.) pkg.
   instant banana
   pudding mix
2 C. whipped
   topping, divided

Arrange ⅔ of the banana slices evenly over bottom of prepared cooled pie crust. In a medium bowl, combine milk, French vanilla pudding mix and banana pudding mix. Beat with a wire whisk until pudding thickens. Fold in ½ cup whipped topping. Pour mixture over bananas in pie crust. Chill in refrigerator at least 3 hours. Before serving, top with remaining 1½ cups whipped topping and ⅓ banana slices. Store in refrigerator.

Strawberry Berry Chiffon Pie

Makes 1 (9″) pie

2 C. fresh strawberries, quartered, divided

2 C. fresh raspberries, divided

1 C. sugar

¼ C. orange juice

2 T. fresh lemon juice

2 tsp. unflavored gelatin

2 C. heavy whipping cream, divided

1 (9") pre-baked pie crust

Additional berries for topping

In a food processor or blender, puree ½ cup strawberries and ½ cup raspberries. Strain berries through a fine sieve into a medium bowl. Add remaining 1½ cups strawberries and 1½ cups raspberries. Stir in sugar. Mix well and set aside. In a small heat resistant bowl, combine orange juice and lemon juice. Sprinkle gelatin over juice and let sit for 5 minutes. Place bowl in a small saucepan of water over low heat. Warm gelatin, stirring frequently, until smooth and clear. Add gelatin mixture to berry mixture. Mix and chill in refrigerator for 20 minutes, until mixture thickens slightly. Meanwhile, in a separate bowl, beat heavy cream to stiff peaks. Fold half of the whipped cream into the berry mixture. Spoon filling into prepared pie crust. Chill in refrigerator at least 2 hours. Before serving, top with remaining half of the whipped cream. Garnish pie with additional berries. Store in refrigerator.

Butter Brickle Banana Pie

Makes 1 (9″) pie

⅓ C. plus 2 T. butter, divided

1⅓ C. sugar, divided

⅓ C. slivered almonds

4 C. half n' half, divided

3 egg yolks

½ C. cornstarch

Pinch of salt

½ tsp. almond extract

1 (9″) pre-baked pie crust

2 bananas, peeled and sliced

1 C. heavy whipping cream

In a heavy saucepan, combine ⅓ cup butter, ⅓ cup sugar and slivered almonds. Bring mixture to a boil over medium heat, stirring constantly, until golden brown. Transfer butter brickle to a lightly greased piece of tin foil to cool. In a medium bowl, combine ¼ cup half n' half and egg yolks. Mix well and set aside. In a separate saucepan, combine remaining 1 cup sugar, cornstarch and pinch of salt. Bring mixture to a simmer over medium heat. Gradually blend in remaining 3¾ cups half n' half. Reduce heat to low and cook mixture, stirring constantly, until thick and steamy. Remove from heat and add 1 cup half n' half mixture to beaten egg yolks, whisking constantly. Pour egg yolk mixture back into saucepan and return to heat. Cook over low heat for about 3 minutes, stirring constantly, being careful not to boil. Remove from heat and stir in remaining 2 tablespoons butter and almond extract. Pour mixture into a medium bowl and cover with plastic wrap. Press plastic wrap onto surface of mixture to prevent skin from

(continued from previous page)

forming. Let mixture cool to room temperature. Break butter brickle into pieces and crush with a rolling pin or in a food processor. Sprinkle half of the butter brickle crumbs into the bottom of prepared pie crust. Place sliced bananas over butter brickle. Spoon room temperature filling evenly over bananas. In a separate bowl, beat heavy cream with a wire whisk to stiff peaks. Spread whipped cream evenly over filling in pie crust. Sprinkle remaining half of butter brickle crumbs over whipped cream. Serve immediately. Store in refrigerator.

Strawberry Jam Pie

Makes 1 (9″) pie

6 C. fresh strawberries, quartered, divided
¾ C. sugar
2 T. cornstarch
2 T. fresh lemon juice
1 (9″) pre-baked pie crust

In a food processor or blender, puree 2 cups strawberries. Strain berries through a fine sieve into a medium bowl and set aside. In a medium saucepan, combine sugar and cornstarch. Stir in lemon juice, mixing until smooth. Gradually stir in pureed strawberries. Cook mixture over medium low heat, stirring constantly, until mixture just boils. Reduce heat until mixture is simmering slowly and cook for 1 minute, stirring constantly. Remove from heat and stir in remaining 4 cups strawberries. Spoon mixture into prepared pie crust. Chill in refrigerator 1 hour, until firm. Store in refrigerator.

Three Layer Chocolate Pie

Makes 1 (9″) pie

2 (1 oz.) squares
semisweet chocolate,
melted

¼ C. sweetened
condensed milk

1 (9″) prepared
chocolate cookie
crumb crust

¾ C. chopped pecans,
toasted*

2 C. milk

2 (3.4 oz.) pkgs. instant
chocolate pudding
mix

1 (8 oz.) container
whipped topping,
divided

In a large bowl, combine melted chocolate squares and sweetened condensed milk. Stir until smooth. Pour into prepared pie crust. Press chopped pecans evenly onto chocolate mixture in crust. Chill in refrigerator for 10 minutes. In a separate bowl, combine milk and chocolate pudding mix. Beat with a wire whisk for 2 minutes, until thickened and smooth. Spread 1½ cups pudding over pecans in pie crust. Fold half of the whipped topping into remaining pudding. Spread mixture evenly over pudding in crust. Top with remaining half of whipped topping. Chill for 3 hours in refrigerator, until set. Store in refrigerator.

* To toast, place chopped pecans in a single layer on a baking sheet. Bake at 350° for approximately 10 minutes or until pecans are golden brown.

Frozen Orange Cream Pie

Makes 1 (9") pie

1 qt. vanilla frozen
  yogurt, softened
½ (12 oz.) can
  frozen orange
  juice concentrate,
  thawed
1 (9") prepared
  graham cracker
  crust

1 (8 oz.) container
  whipped topping,
  optional
Orange slices,
  optional

In a large bowl, using a mixer at medium speed, combine vanilla yogurt and orange juice concentrate. Spread mixture evenly into prepared pie crust. Chill in freezer for 4 hours, until firm. If desired, top with whipped topping and orange slices before serving. Store in freezer.

Raspberry Ice Cream Pie

Makes 1 (9") pie

⅔ C. boiling orange juice
1 (3 oz.) pkg. raspberry flavored gelatin
1 C. vanilla ice cream

1 (8 oz.) container whipped topping, divided
1 C. fresh raspberries, optional
1 (9") Oreo pie crust

In a large bowl, combine boiling orange juice and raspberry gelatin. Stir at least 3 minutes, until gelatin is completely dissolved. Gradually add vanilla ice cream, stirring constantly, until ice cream is melted and mixture is smooth. Stir in ½ cup whipped topping. If desired, gently stir in raspberries. Chill in refrigerator until mixture slightly mounds when dropped from a spoon. Spoon mixture into prepared pie crust. Refrigerate 3 hours or freeze until firm. Before serving, spread remaining whipped topping over pie. Store in freezer.

Frozen Chocolate-Mint Pie

Makes 1 (9″) pie

2 C. whipped topping
1 (7.5 oz.) jar
 marshmallow
 creme
1 tsp. mint extract
4 to 6 drops green
 food coloring

15 thin chocolate
 mint wafers,
 crumbled
1 (9″) Oreo pie crust
Fresh mint and
 chocolate curls for
 garnish, optional

In a large bowl, combine whipped topping and marshmallow creme with a wire whisk until well blended. Add mint extract and green food coloring. Mix well. Gently stir in crumbled mint wafers. Spoon filling into prepared pie crust. Freeze at least 4 hours, until firm. If desired, before serving garnish pie with fresh mint and chocolate curls. Store in freezer.

Apricot Fluff Pie

Makes 1 (9″) pie

2 T. butter or
  margarine
¼ C. corn syrup
1 C. chocolate chips
2 C. Special K cereal
1 (15 to 15.5 oz.) can
  apricot halves in
  juice

1 (3 oz.) pkg. orange
  flavored gelatin
2 C. whipped topping

In a medium saucepan over low heat, melt butter, corn syrup and chocolate chips. Stir constantly until mixture is smooth. Remove from heat and stir in Special K cereal, stirring until well coated. Press mixture evenly into bottom and up sides of a greased 8″ or 9″ pie pan. Chill in refrigerator. Drain apricots, reserving 1 cup juice. Reserve 8 apricot halves and set aside. Cut remaining apricot halves into small pieces and set aside. In a small saucepan, bring reserved apricot juice to a boil over medium heat. Pour hot juice into a large bowl and add gelatin, stirring until dissolved. Let mixture chill and slightly thicken. Whip chilled gelatin until thick and foamy. Gently fold in whipped topping and apricot pieces. Spoon filling into prepared pie crust and chill for 1 hour in refrigerator, until set. Before serving, arrange reserved apricot halves on pie. If desired, garnish with additional whipped topping. Store in refrigerator.

Citrus Chiffon Pie

Makes 1 (9″) pie

1 (¼ oz.) pkg.
  unflavored gelatin
½ C. plus ⅓ C. sugar,
  divided
Pinch of salt
4 eggs, separated
½ C. lemon juice
½ C. orange juice
½ tsp. grated lemon
  peel

½ tsp. grated orange
  peel
1 (9″) prepared graham
  cracker crust
½ C. whipped topping
Fresh mint and orange
  slices for garnish,
  optional

In a medium saucepan, combine gelatin, ½ cup sugar and salt. In a medium bowl, combine egg yolks, lemon juice, orange juice and ¼ cup water. Beat until smooth. Stir mixture into gelatin mixture in saucepan. Cook mixture over medium heat, stirring constantly, until mixture boils. Remove from heat and add lemon peel and orange peel. Chill, stirring occasionally, until mixture mounds slightly when dropped from a spoon. In a separate bowl, beat egg whites until foamy. Gradually add remaining ⅓ cup sugar, beating until stiff. Fold in gelatin mixture. Pour all into prepared pie crust. Chill in refrigerator until firm. Before serving, spread whipped topping over pie. If desired, garnish with fresh mint leaves and orange slices. Store in refrigerator.

Cranberry Parfait Pie

Makes 1 (9″) pie

1 C. cranberry juice
2 (3 oz.) pkgs. strawberry flavored gelatin
1 C. whole berry cranberry sauce
½ C. vanilla ice cream
1 (9″) prepared graham cracker crust
½ C. heavy whipping cream
¼ C. sugar
1 tsp. vanilla

In a medium saucepan, heat cranberry juice over low heat. Stir in strawberry gelatin, mixing until dissolved. Cook for about 15 to 20 minutes, stirring occasionally, until thickened. Remove from heat and transfer to a medium mixing bowl. Beat mixture at medium low speed until fluffy. In a blender or food processor, finely chop the whole cranberry sauce. Mix in gelatin mixture and vanilla ice cream until well blended. Transfer blended mixture into prepared pie crust. Chill in refrigerator for 2 to 3 hours. In a medium bowl, whip heavy cream, sugar and vanilla. Before serving, spread mixture over filling in pie crust. Store in freezer.

Saucy Toffee Ice Cream Pie

Makes 1 (9″) pie

½ gal. vanilla ice
  cream, softened,
  divided
1 (9″) prepared
  graham cracker
  crust
1½ C. English toffee
  bits, divided

1½ C. sugar
1 C. evaporated milk
½ C. butter
¼ C. light corn syrup
Pinch of salt

Spoon half of the vanilla ice cream in prepared pie crust. Sprinkle ½ cup toffee bits over ice cream. Spoon remaining ice cream over toffee bits. Cover and freeze for 4 to 6 hours, until firm. In a medium saucepan, combine sugar, evaporated milk, butter, light corn syrup and salt. Cook over low heat, stirring constantly, until mixture boils. Boil and stir for 1 minute. Remove from heat and stir in remaining 1 cup toffee bits. Let cool, stirring occasionally. Before serving, drizzle sauce over pie pieces. Store pie in freezer and sauce in refrigerator.

Orange Cooler Pie

Makes 1 (9″) pie

¼ C. butter, melted

1⅔ C. crushed
graham crackers

½ C. plus 3 T. sugar,
divided

½ C. half n' half

½ (12 oz.) can
frozen orange
juice concentrate,
thawed

1 tsp. cinnamon

½ tsp. nutmeg

2 C. vanilla ice cream,
softened

Whipped topping
and orange slices
for garnish

In a large bowl, combine melted butter, crushed graham crackers and 3 tablespoons sugar. Mix well and press into the bottom and up sides of a 9″ pie pan. In a medium mixing bowl, combine half n' half and remaining ½ cup sugar. Beat for 2 minutes. Add orange juice concentrate, cinnamon and nutmeg. Beat for 1 minute. Add vanilla ice cream and beat for an additional 2 minutes. Pour filling into prepared pie crust. Freeze 4 hours or overnight. If desired, before serving garnish with whipped topping and orange slices. Store in freezer.

Fruit Smoothie Cheesecake

Makes 1 (9″) pie

1 C. whole
   strawberries
1 banana, peeled
2 (8 oz.) pkgs. cream
   cheese, softened
⅓ C. sugar
1 (8 oz.) container
   whipped topping

1 (9″) prepared
   graham cracker
   crust
Additional
   strawberries for
   garnish, optional

In a food processor or blender, puree strawberries and banana. In a large mixing bowl, combine softened cream cheese and sugar at medium speed until well blended. Gently stir in pureed strawberry and banana mixture and whipped topping. Spoon mixture into prepared crust. Freeze 4 hours or overnight, until firm. Let stand at room temperature 1 hour before serving. If desired, garnish with fresh strawberries. Store in refrigerator or freezer.

Heavenly Orange Cheesecake

Makes 1 (9″) pie

1 pkg. unflavored
gelatin
½ C. orange juice
3 (8 oz.) pkgs. cream
cheese, softened
¾ C. sugar
1 (12 oz.) container
whipped topping

1 T. grated orange
peel
1 (9″) prepared
chocolate cookie
crumb crust

In a small saucepan, combine gelatin and orange juice over low heat. Stir until gelatin is dissolved. In a medium mixing bowl, combine softened cream cheese and sugar at medium speed until well blended. Gradually add gelatin mixture, beating well after each addition. Chill in refrigerator about 30 minutes, until slightly thickened. Gently fold in whipped topping and orange peel. Pour mixture into prepared crust. Chill in refrigerator for 3 hours, until firm. Store in refrigerator.

German Sweet Chocolate Pie

Makes 1 (9″) pie

½ (8 oz.) pkg. Baker's
  German sweet
  chocolate
5 T. milk, divided
½ (8 oz.) pkg. cream
  cheese, cubed and
  softened
2 T. sugar

1 (8 oz.) container
  whipped topping
1 (9″) prepared graham
  cracker crust
Whipped topping and
  shaved chocolate for
  garnish

In a large microwave-safe bowl, combine sweet chocolate and 2 tablespoons milk. Microwave for 1½ to 2 minutes, stirring after 45 seconds, until chocolate is almost melted. Remove from microwave and stir until chocolate is completely melted. In a medium bowl, combine softened cream cheese cubes, sugar and remaining 3 tablespoons milk. Beat mixture with a wire whisk until well blended. Chill in refrigerator for 10 minutes. Gently fold in whipped topping until smooth. Spoon mixture into prepared pie crust. Freeze 4 hours, until firm. Let stand at room temperature 15 minutes before serving. Garnish with additional whipped topping and shaved chocolate. Store in refrigerator.

Lemon Berry Pie

Makes 1 (9″) pie

½ (8 oz.) pkg. cream cheese, cubed and softened

2 C. plus 1 T. milk, divided

1 T. sugar

2 tsp. grated lemon peel

1 T. fresh lemon juice

1 (8 oz.) container whipped topping, divided

1 (9″) prepared graham cracker crust

2 C. fresh strawberries, quartered

2 (3.4 oz.) pkgs. instant lemon pudding mix

In a medium bowl, combine softened cream cheese cubes, 1 tablespoon milk and sugar. Beat with a wire whisk until smooth. Stir in lemon peel and lemon juice. Gently fold in 1½ cups whipped topping. Spread mixture evenly over bottom of prepared pie crust. Press strawberries into cream cheese layer in pie crust. In a large bowl, combine remaining 2 cups milk and pudding mix. Beat with a wire whisk for 1 minute. Gently stir in 1 cup whipped topping. Spoon mixture over strawberries in crust. Chill in refrigerator for 4 hours, until set. Before serving, spread remaining whipped topping over pie. Store in refrigerator.

Index

Cookies

Bars

Pies